T0359219

WRITERS

ON

WRITERS

Published in partnership with

STATE LIBRARY
VICTORIA
What's your story?

THE UNIVERSITY OF
MELBOURNE

WRITERS
NAM
LE
ON
DAVID
MALOUF
WRITERS

Black Inc.

For Ché

Published by Black Inc.
in association with the University of Melbourne and State Library Victoria.

Black Inc., an imprint of Schwartz Publishing Pty Ltd
Level 1, 221 Drummond Street, Carlton Victoria 3053 Australia
enquiries@blackincbooks.com   www.blackincbooks.com

State Library Victoria
328 Swanston Street, Melbourne Victoria 3000 Australia
www.slv.vic.gov.au

The University of Melbourne
Parkville Victoria 3010 Australia
www.unimelb.edu.au

9781760640392 (hardback)
9781743820926 (ebook)

A catalogue record for this
book is available from the
National Library of Australia

Cover design by Peter Long and Akiko Chan
Typesetting by Akiko Chan
Photograph of Nam Le: Dave Tacon
Photograph of David Malouf: Dominic Lorrimer/Fairfax Media

Printed in China by 1010 Printing

PRIME

S trange, that I remember only the mornings. Or maybe it was all a single morning, all those high school years – dark chill runny-nosed morning, shock of school uniform starch against the skin. Kerbs and platforms, buses and trains and trams and traffic lights. I was a scholarship kid and never felt like I belonged there and maybe I made sure to make it so – blocked myself out till pretty much insensible. Melbourne Grammar (1991–1996) was bluestone shadow, navy blue and paler blue recurring, faces floating against rain and a sort of drowned light. It was sports fields gone green and wet, galleys of wooden desks and the always reverberant voice in those wood-filled rooms calling *Anyone? Anyone at all?*, naming names – Sibree, Hooper, Dinning, Frye, Downing – fathers' names, patriarchs' names. The light that light of air just after rain. Classrooms full of wood and plastered drywalls, nylon charts and corked pinboards and washed and chalk-clotted blackboards, all barely masking the cold, sounding, ancient stone beneath. That was high school. Mood dream, time tolled through the body.

But dreams are multi-registral. They can be all mood and still take in all sorts of other stuff. They admit whatever comes to mind. My mind at the time was mucked up: by hormones, by classroom codes, by inchoate insecurities and ambitions, by the disjunctions – language, ethics, expectation, allegiance – between school and home. Nothing was given. What was *home*, anyway, and what *away*? What I knew was this: I was most at home when reading, when being taken away by words.

I read in English. (Both tenses apply.) For a while there I read mostly poetry, which seemed to ratify or at least dignify my outsized feelings. School, as everyone knows, is where books go to get sterilised, so I was lucky to have English teachers who let me read outside the curriculum. Palgrave and Norton were my boon companions. Human-wise, my best friend was Ché, a bawdy, brainy country boy who'd managed to land a spectacular *triple* scholarship (tuition, music, boarding). He played piano. I read poetry, and then I wrote it, and then he read it. He was my first *real* reader – by which I mean he proclaimed my talent as amongst the brightest that had ever blazed across our or any firmament. We were big on ranking talent, on absorbing and contriving distinctions. Yeats over Keats, Rilke over Rimbaud. Hopkins over

Donne, but only just. We argued intensely and violently when I said Tennyson and he Blake. Or maybe it was the other way around. We were very serious; we persuaded our Lit teacher to accept a joint essay qua duet: Ché at the grand piano in the gym riffing off Ravel and Berg while I stood alongside, reciting rip-offs of Eliot and Pound.

We were not popular.

What we'd realised, though, was there could be agency in exclusion. If we were going to be outsiders, we would decide outside what. To hell with friendship groups stretching back twelve years plus, to family alums and fundraising networks, homes in Toorak and holidays in Noosa, to men's eights and first elevens and eighteens – instead, we would camp on the periphery of ye olde *haute culture*, importuning ourselves upon its canons and classics.

This, of course, was (is) classic cringe. A condition of always choosing the other side. Putting yourself on the wrong side. But so we chose. The dead over the living. The old over the new. The white over the coloured. The European over the Antipodean, the international over the Australian. Always the proscribed over the prescribed (or, in one of English's archest contronyms — and how couldn't you love this language? — the sanctioned over the sanctioned). At the time, post-Bicentennial, there was a grand push to triumphalise Australian literature, so even as we submitted to the Ozlit foisted on us at school, we saw those books for what they were: scabs, labouring to shore up the shibboleths of shoddy nationalism. We scorned them. They were substandard. They were, to use perhaps the most cutting put-down of our schoolboy sociolect, 'try-hard'.

And then we got where we were going. Assigned via VCE reading list: *Remembering Babylon*, David Malouf. An Australian book about Australian settlement by an Australian author. And here, of course, is where I've been going. This sleek, slim book – readable in an afternoon – was *good*. Not a whiff of affirmative action. It shook our snobberies: here was a very-much-alive half-Lebanese writer (from provincial Brisbane, no less) producing English-language writing of the very first order. (We spoke like this.) And in prose, not poetry. The poetry was *in* the prose; it stayed and sprung its rhythms, chorded its ideas, concentrated its images. Every other novel claims to be written in 'poetic prose'; the real thing, when you come across it, is actually shocking. It torques your reading brain (neuroimaging confirms this), drafts your breath, excites and exhausts your eye and ear. It's as taxing as it is exultative. *Remembering Babylon*, while being syllabus-bait for its Big Ideas, was acutely for me a sentence-level novel.

What does this mean? Isn't any novel (and its evoked ideas) only and always made of sentences? Yes … and yes … but only a writer attuned to the molecular level of syllable and sound can understand how profoundly ideas inhere in their inspiriting expressions. See, e.g., the book's last paragraph:

> It glows in fullness till the tide is high and the light almost, but not quite, unbearable, as the moon plucks at our world and all the waters of the earth ache towards it, and the light, running in fast now, reaches the edges of the shore, just so far in its order, and all the muddy margin of the bay is alive, and in a line of running

fire all the outline of the vast continent
appears, in touch now with its other life.

Critics have maligned this passage for its
transcendentalism, but who could deny its
grace? Its ambition of register – the biblically
inflected tone and parataxis; the gorgeous
mimesis of its tidal ebb – or its register of ambition – the cosmic, vatic scope of its concern, fast
erupting through space and time? The subject
is light and light lies all through it. Reading
this for the first time, Ché and I, as propensely
hostile as we were, couldn't but cede. Here was
language that drew meaning out of music, of
echo, silence. That communicated before it
meant. Here was lyricism that neither beat up
nor blenched at the sublime but treated it as a
necessary aspect of ordinary life. Most of all,
here was a confidence that seemed to flex its way
serenely through any niggles of cringe.

Here was a way forward.

~

Twenty-odd years have passed since then. In that time I've re-read *Remembering Babylon* maybe a half-dozen times. There was a stage – when it mattered to me – I'd go around touting that book as the Great Australian Novel/ Bunyip. Since then I've also read pretty much all of Malouf's other output. His books may be slim but there are lots of them.

The man and his books have been praised and puffed and premiated and I think this is fine and right but I'm not really interested, as a rule, in writing encomia. Besides, so much has been written about his body of work, from the expected angles, through the expected prisms, I'd feel redundant reprising those staples here. I say 'expected' because Malouf is adept at slyly steering his eponymous studies: not only through interviews, essays and lectures but in his imaginative writing itself, where themes and ideas are often elegantly laid out as though inviting cut-paste-and-tabbing in academic papers. When it comes to critical responses, Malouf's work (perhaps more than any other Australian writer's) has truly lopped a thousand trees.

So what am I doing here? To ask a writer to write 'on' another writer is (for this writer, at least) to activate acute prepositional anxiety. No syntactical unit is asked to be more load-bearing. If a preposition between two nouns fixes them in relationship to (with?) each other, the way I read that single word – 'on' – may well determine my relationship to David Malouf.

'On' means 'about', of course, by way of exposition or interpretation. But it can also connote spatiality: am I on top of, supported by Malouf – standing on his shoulders, as it were?

Or am I writing 'on' as in 'over' him, my words laid over his words, redacting, even replacing them? Do I intend us to be contiguous or coincident? Coeval, or clear as possible of temporal overlay? Am I 'on' Malouf as a function of following 'after' him, on his heels? (Attenborough springs to mind – to be 'on' something is also to capture the instant of attack: now the lion is on the gazelle, the cheetah the wildebeest ...)

Nothing so dramatic here. What follows is much as what's gone before: a thinking out loud, a setting down of thinking. Not overwriting but personal annotation. Just one more view from the margins.

~

In the time since I first read *Remembering Babylon* (as I embarked upon my own writing), David Malouf has become for me something of a paragon of praxis. I've never met the man, never seen him in person. (I'm trying to write this as though he were dead.) But there is an intimacy – an oft-occurring word in Malouf studies – between us. That the intimacy is one-way only makes it more dependable.

I guess I'm supposed to spell it out. It feels self-serving and self-exposing to assume any connection at all, but here goes. Like Malouf, I started in poetry. Like him, I'd like to think, I've never left it – even when moving into fiction. Poetry is the weather, the prevailing conditions. When I learned recently that he too used scansion notation to meter out prose, I felt – no kidding – less of a freak in the world.

I feel kinship with the unapologetic nature of Malouf's learning, his reading – *his* chosen networks of literary kinship. With the dignity of his extraordinary (and evolving) erudition. The naturalness of his assumption of inheritance.

His lines lead back to Europe, this is fact. His writing comes up fulgent from immersion in Western classicism. Reading Malouf, you get the sense at times he thinks the entirety of human concern was satisfactorily carved up between Homer and Hesiod three thousand years ago, and everything since has been interpolation and ornament. At times, I think I agree.

But we inherit more than the work. We inherit the method that can vitiate the work. That can even void it. Like Malouf, I'm a student of Western philosophy. I honour the Western approaches of intrinsic scepticism, self-critical inquiry, uncertainty. I hew, as hard as I can, to epistemic humility. These are the same approaches that have, it's important to note, successfully prosecuted the Western canon for its perpetuations of imperialism and privilege, its cultural genocides – it's not too much to call them that – that have ripped from the world countless works, actual and potential, that dared associate with the wrong sex, race, creed, caste, class, colony – you name it. Surely no serious thinker denies this. Nor that the work that remains (overwhelmingly by dead white men) is conditioned by, and complicit in, its milieu. Nor that this stigma is still perceptible – on the page, and between the lines. But I've never met a serious thinker who considers this work to be therefore worthless. We are not so rich in art to deplore what we have merely because it is not what we might have had. Having been deprived of female, or black, or baseborn Shakespeares and Socrateses, must we now deprive ourselves of the ones we do have? Is it not possible to acknowledge their worth, critique the context that begat them, and then go out of our way – out of our skin – to find, encourage, value and include works by and about all those people who all this time have been systematically 'othered'?

All this feels rudimentary. Unremarkable. But in our shared, splintering moment, nothing can be said to go without saying. Basic things beg belabouring. So here's one thing: Culture is complex. Another: The 'culture wars' have nothing to do with culture. The real casualty of these wars is truth; culture itself is AWOL. Culture can't be trusted, after all, to shoot straight; it's changeable, capricious, tightly coiled, better at asking questions than taking orders. Its units are highly individuated and overly subjective. On the worst parts of the right, 'culture warriors' worship 'Western culture' only as far as they can weaponise it. The worst of the left, in response – pursuing its pet strategy of self-righteous self-loathing – relinquishes 'Western culture' to the right. (That culture in toto could be posited as partisan shows how degraded the discourse has become.) Under this set-up, 'West' becomes metonymical for 'wrong'. To defend it is to defend only its sins; to commend it – any facet of its thoughts, ideals, institutions or art – is to condone – lock, stock & barrel – the whole atrocity. Better, then, if you're a fellow traveller, to steer clear, shut up.

Malouf doesn't do this. For this I admire him. He owns his occidentalism, in all its con- tradictions and culpabilities. And for this, his name, of late, has come under faint stain. For being a tad too … cultivated … too belletris- tic … for hanging out, basically, with a non grata crowd of dead white guys. The kicker was his acceptance of a lecture invitation from the Ramsay Centre for Western Civilisation, a new outfit which *subsequently*, on a separate matter, waded into the culture wars and deservedly ended up in hot water. The lecture itself? David Malouf extolling the complication of women in ancient Greek drama. Haul up guillotine blade!

The man is too dignified to answer snideries in public (and he certainly doesn't need me to defend him) but I'm not so bound and I'm stumped for his sake and I want to say this: smear by association is easy. When done from tribe, it can also feel oxytocin-good. Even easier is to abhor writers and their works – whether individual writers or their entire matrices of influence – when you haven't read them; when, in fact, your tribe actively rewards you for maintaining ignorance. You're merely de-platforming a problematics, the lingo goes (even if the only platform at issue is your brain, the only issue at stake your intellectual integrity). None of this is new. It is the craven logic of bullying. The agora, where speech is meant to be most free, has always attracted mobs. And the kind of rhetoric deployed against Malouf and his impugned alliance with 'Western civilisation' – argument *ad ignorantiam* (from ignorance), *ad populum* (appealing to group belief), *ad verecundiam* (via self-proclaimed 'authority'), *ad nauseam* (by repetition), *ad baculum* (made under threat) – constitutes, ironically, a greatest hits of Western suasion. Calling it out in Latin makes it insufferable, but no less true.

One more thing. This is also a logic of purity and contamination. And we should know better. Nothing complex is pure; the wanting it so has led to unspeakable, immeasurable suffering. We should know better. Those who crave purity – who would tell us what may be read, and by whom, and who may write what, and how, who would sort us into silos of identity and then, worst of all, vacate the 'good' for the 'correct' – should, by their own argument *ad absurdum*, have nothing more to do with the written word. After all, what could be more impure, more steeped in blood, than written language itself – a technology only invented to keep account of grain and slaves, and then to codify the placations of God to keep the oppressed oppressed? How many lies have been told in it, how many deaths ordered, lives destroyed? 'There is no document of civilization which is not at the same time a document of barbarism', writes Walter Benjamin, and this doesn't even go to the philological violence *within* language, the merciless miscegenation, the way words, meanings and usages – all of which bear witness to real human lives – are supplanted, marginalised and effaced. A dictionary is a site of massacre. A language is a living corruption.

And, I happen to think, it is the best thing we have. And I think Malouf would agree with me.

~

What else?

His affable humanism, how he errs into compassion rather than condescension. I aspire to this. That the self is protean, provisional, makes it no less sacrosanct. Auden, to whom we both owe early and enduring faith, writes in *Horae Canonicae* that we should 'bless what there is for being'. This is as close as I come to creed. This is what I see in Malouf's eidetic writing. We share, I think, a sense of wonder towards a world that is both sui generis and palimpsestic, sacred with beauty and mystery – against which epiphany serves not as literary reaction but as dialectic of being alive. The world makes us. We can, in our small way, through our writing, perform the mimic miracle. Make a new world.

Underwriting and entangled in all this is consciousness. The sine qua non of all the rest of it. Of thinking and feeling, being and becoming, making and minding. Consciousness, as well – to belabour the point – is complex or it is nothing. The question of how we should go about (failing to) articulate it lies at the very heart of literature. That Malouf puts it at the heart of his body of work makes his work vital for me. When Malouf invokes 'seriousness' – which he does often – he is talking, I believe, about morality. A good-faithed, ongoing attempt at articulation.

Consciousness is our entire access – it opens us to the world, to each other. But it also confirms us in our solipsism. It locks us in; language offers no parole. None of us can escape (or even parenthesise) our own consciousness to experience another's. None of us is available to each other in this essential way. Every common reality we think we share actually consists in convention and conjecture, axiom and supposition. (Think back to those dopey undergrad moots where, wait for it ... what if *red* for you looked *blue* to me ...)

Turned inward, consciousness proves to be no more clarifying. It is almost all unseen, all unknown – all process and no phenomena. Self-consciousness, per Malouf in *Ransom*, 'makes us strange to ourselves and darkly divided'. We are not meant, perhaps, to presume ourselves to scan. Certainly we do not have clean hands, nor clear mind, with which to properly do so.

Last year he died, Ché, my old, young friend: London, suspicious circs, autopsy. It was the first day of the year and I found out on Facebook, the whole thing shot through with the sly feel of a joke. For so long we'd been living on different continents; distance had preserved our friendship in its formative attitudes: we were permanently outsiders looking in, permanently aspirants to unscalable tradition. His death brought up all the eulogic chestnuts – live each day as if, life being short – but more power-fully, more brutally, it resurfaced all our shared schoolboy ardencies. Beauty and truth. Excel-lence. Seriousness. Even writing these words, a wryness creeps in – an ironic reflex. How did this happen? How had we – had I – allowed these standards to become embarrassing? Was it *because* we'd chosen self-exile for their sake that we then felt obliged – out of some weird pride or petulance – to distance ourselves from the very solace we'd sought in them?

Malouf's first novel, *Johnno*, recounts a friendship between two boys that also starts in school and ends when one of them dies suddenly. The friendship is charged, complicated, built on Australian cringe and the bulwarks of European culture. After Johnno dies, the narrator, nicknamed Dante (of course), reflects on his old school's honour boards for the war-dead:

> And just reading off the places where they fell, Ypres, Mons, Gallipoli, Pozièrs, Bullecourt, evoked a peculiar atmosphere of golden splendour and colonial chivalry that we might have longed for like a broken dream. Their deaths were both tragedy and fulfilment.

That Europe's 'golden splendour' is washed by blood, waxed by colonial depredation, makes those lives lost at Ypres, Gallipoli, Pozièrs (and how right was Hemingway that in war only the names of places hold dignity?) no less dead.

That Europe is a broken dream makes it no less meaningful. Johnno dies and Dante goes to visit his mum. There, it is she who comforts him: Johnno is happy, she assures him. 'He's with Nietzsche and Schopenhauer.'

Whereof one cannot speak, thereof one must be silent. In the same war, in his twenties, on the heels of Schopenhauer and Nietzsche, Wittgenstein ended his *Tractatus Logico-Philosophicus* with this proposition. The *Tractatus* itself, he considered, went on to end every problem in logic. But where logic ends, literature begins. ('*The limits of my language* mean the limits of my world.') If you believe this, you must believe that to enlarge the possibilities of language – against the necessities of silence – is to enlarge the world. I have come to believe, with Malouf, that any serious literature – any real articulation of consciousness in language – must set, each time, its main strategy against silence: which salients to yield, which to approach in a 'spirit of play', how best to mass and mobilise words against negative capability. Ellipse, error, illusion. We press on, seeking ways out of our selves that do not exist, failing to say what we cannot say. This is, for Malouf (and for me), the big game, the end game. This is the labour of his life. We are privileged to watch.

PIGEON

A couple of years ago, I accepted an invitation to be a writer-in-residence at the University of Wyoming. These gigs typically involve a little teaching, a little money, a little time to write. Just before I flew over, I was informed that in addition to my pedagogical duties, I had been slated to appear at a number of events across the state advocating for refugee settlement.

I hadn't been asked first.

These events entailed being flown in a small single-engine plane to deliver pro-refugee talks in fairly conservative places (in one town, the cops arrested a rabble-rouser who'd put out a podcast call inciting violence), guest-slotting a 'social justice' book club, and doing a bunch

of media. The worst of it was a PBS TV bit.
I could've said no but I didn't, I said this:

> I was a refugee. My family was involved
> in the Vietnam War and ... when things
> went downhill, we, like millions of other
> Vietnamese, fled the country ... When
> we were in trouble, Australia let us in and
> took us in and looked after us. They had
> no reason, really, to do it; they had a lot
> of reasons not to. They didn't know us.
> They didn't owe us anything ... It still
> does boggle me when I think about that,
> and it's not really something that grati-
> tude can cover. It's too big for that. But
> what it does bring home to me is [that]
> beyond the politics and the policies and
> the very legitimate notions of sovereignty,
> border protection, of cultural preserva-
> tion, there's still this project of very simple

grace – of just helping people who need help even though you don't owe them any help. And that, to me, meant everything when we needed it.

Predictable stuff, right? Most people, I reckon, from left and right alike, would find these sentiments unobjectionable, even agreeable. Most people would be confused by my own reaction to them – for any time I see this clip, I come away with a wretched feeling – a mixture of unease and ire and self-directed scorn. That I did it to myself – let myself do it to myself – makes it harder to bear.

What exactly did I do?

I allowed myself to be used. I became a mouthpiece. I took in vain my plural self to spruik a singular, flat, facile politics. In part, I did it because I agreed with the politics – pinned down, *of course* I thought/think the US should be resettling Syrian refugees – but my problem was with being pinned down, coerced into answering *that* question without being free to question the question's underpinnings, its mess of historical, political and ethical consensions. None of the terms were open to me. How could I in all conscience argue for the stateless, for example, when, to me, the very consensus of the Westphalian nation-state feels unconscionable – a spur to hate and horror? How could I make a case for immigration when I hold the very concept of territorial sovereignty responsible for encoding the world's deadliest asymmetries? A state is *a priori* an exclusionary mechanism. It ransoms the human need for belonging against the human wont to tribalism and xenophobia. It justifies the self-interest that justifies its statehood – ouroboros, ad infinitum. A state sets limits and conditions – that is its deal.

All politics is border politics. Sovereignty doesn't mean much without someone else to shove it to.

On top of that, I loathed the whole set-up – I couldn't help feeling a familiar vein of bad faith running through all these good intentions. Social justice is easy when it's low-cost, high-return. Wasn't this just another way we could all broadcast our progressivism without forfeiting our exceptionalism? (No pro-refugee activist there was proposing open borders.) Wasn't this just another neoliberal application of virtue, whereby we could accrue socio-cultural capital through the Having of Opinions without having, ourselves, to forgo any economic capital or comfort? Guilt as vehicle for vanity?

And all done via the amiable, earnest Asian-Australian guest (an '*Eminent* Writer-in-Residence', no less) who had *been there*, and even written about it!

This, of course, was the other thing. I had taken in vain my writing self. I had used language in a way that was antithetical to what I ask of my writing: that it come from me, and carry some of my life, and convey my truth (including its uncertainties, ambiguities and antinomies) in as true a form as I can find, wherever it might lead me. What I delivered instead was a maudlin Hallmark ad for my 'sponsors', pitched intuitively at the level of coddling and congratulation. I took an issue about which I have insoluble feelings and – having no opportunity to think it down through writing – instead boiled it down to literal propaganda. What candour might have been in it (and of course, in a way, I meant every word) was made performative by camera and context – I felt myself false even while saying what I meant.

At bottom, the failure that wounded me most, I think, was my deference. To the brazen assumption that because I had been a refugee, I would be willing to be identified as a refugee, I would be willing to be defined as a refugee, I would be in support of refugees (whatever that meant), I would be willing to speak in support of refugees. I did what was expected of me. In doing so, I essentialised not only myself but all refugees (who, I know, are as variable, irrational and prejudicial as any other people, including on refugee-related topics). I spoke for others when I wasn't even truly speaking for myself. We refugees are already trapped in a condescending narrative that promotes asylum as destiny; I failed to resist the denouement that ascribes destiny to character.

~

That moment has come back to me over and over again. It's taken some time for me to realise its connection to this essay: it's to do with sovereignty, but of a different kind – personal, artistic, closer in spirit to Bartleby's 'I would prefer not to' or Stephen Dedalus's '*non serviam*'. A sovereignty that recognises that all author-ity – under state or religion or tribe, or even under 'self-evident' abstractions like legitimacy, public good, or moral or civic duty – is coercive in the absence of clear consent. And consent, obviously, can never be clear in a world wholly consisting of 'facts on the ground'.

Which brings me to David Malouf. Over a long career, he seems, somehow, to have pre-served – with natural lightness of touch – this personal, artistic sovereignty for himself.

He is ethnically half-Lebanese (with some Portuguese strained in for good measure), of immigrant stock, yet has for decades elided these aspects of identity to little note and no fuss. (I cannot understand how, even accounting for generational differences, he's managed this.) He's gay but has also managed to stop this from becoming seasonal grist for the queer studies mill. A former academic himself, he must understand that such openings are enticements to academic spits: once stuck, writers can end up turned eternally on the same skewer, basted in the same sauce. Famously private, Malouf has nevertheless intimated enough about himself in his work to ward off too much off-grid digging.

Most impressive to me is his composure; his disregard for fashion or recency (and his collateral disquiet towards contemporary literary 'scenes'); his comfort in his self and his place in the world. Reading him, you find yourself in an exchange with the courteous stranger at the party who, while speaking to you, looks over neither your shoulder nor his own. He eschews labels and allegiances, schools and groups and movements ('a mug's game, a mugger's game', he's called all that). Around about the time my book was published, I came across a quote from him in a newspaper article: 'I totally reject the idea of being representative in any way.'

Yes!

From the first, Malouf has gone his own way. It's an ethos so marked it rises to the status of an ethic. In literal terms, it's meant spending substantial time in England and 'a place in Tuscany' (not quite as idyllic as it sounds, but still . . .). In literary terms, it's meant a restlessness, a searchingness of genre, form and subject that led early (and unimaginative) reviewers to note that his books seemed written by different people. 'You do what you do, the way you do it', Malouf said in that article, 'out of a kind of necessity.'

I know something about labels. My book consisted of short stories that ranged, fairly widely, across settings, styles and subjects. That was what my necessity looked like then. The reviews, mostly positive, were also mostly complicit in common reference to my ethno-nationality – as though no estimation of the work could keep without the seal of the author's status as 'Vietnamese-Australian'. I expected this – even anticipated it in the meta-fictional first story of the collection. And of course I appreciate that context matters, that fiction is scored by both its maker and its making, and that interpreting these marks can be instructive, even enlightening. Proust, notes Malouf (while keeping his own mind), 'is in no doubt that a contemporary writer's life will be known and is part of the text'.

But how has 'life' become so unquestionably

shorthanded – short-changed – into 'identity'? Why should, say, the work of 'ethnic' writers – now that overt orientalisation is out of fashion – remain charged with extra onuses of representation, explanation and authenticity? 'Vietnam' is a Western war. Is it actually impossible for a work by a 'Vietnamese' writer in the West to be evaluated without this unifocal historical knowingness? Without presumed psychodramatic intimacy? Without a framework of imputed, all-smothering victimhood? Auden writes, 'Of any poem written by someone else, my first demand is that it be good.' This is how the writers I know and respect talk about writing – in private. (And yes, we know 'good' is a contested, contingent term.) My naïve hope, I guess, was for my work to be judged the same way in public, unbeholden to the cultural diktat that the more 'marginal' a writer's face, or place of origin, the more central it must be in the commentary. That way lies special pleading – and special treatment.

If literature has a nemesis, it is instrumentalism – the approach that treats it as a tool, values it not for its own sake but as a means to an extrinsic end. This is, I realise now, the language of Kantian metaphysics. Humans are to be treated as ends in themselves, never as means to an end. It makes sense to me that art might warrant the same imperative as people. 'Identity' is not nothing, but it's not everything. What it is – how much it matters – is something for case-by-case consideration. (Another imperative that applies as profoundly to all serious art.) Yes, the system is rigged. It's built on the circular, stupefying logic of 'entry by admission only', which, for so many, for so long, has meant off-limits, no-go, maybe-next-time. But for those of us who have spent our lives fighting for cultural space, respect, autonomy, equity – the last thing we need is for our accession, if and when it comes, to be asterisked. The system wants us to want to belong, at almost any price. We owe it to ourselves to want more.

One term at school, I was chosen as bell ringer. This memory still shines through the murk. I remember the thrill of possessing the empty corridors and courtyards with cause, singled out, special, bearing pass and power to end the given period. I was in charge of all that freedom. I would wait as long as I dared, then swing the rope knotted to the thick brass tongue, swing it hard and regular and skullbreak-strong against the bronze rim.

~

I know something about labels, or my parents do. What follows is a bit patchy, in the way of family histories; I can't entirely vouch for it. In fact, I can barely stand to write it. I don't like to write about personal things in non-fictional mode; the truth feels harder to get to. Yeats said, 'All that is personal soon rots; it must be packed in ice or salt.' He was talking about the formal conventions of lyric but let's allow the poet some play: ice hardens the heart, salt poisons – irrevocably – the razed city.

Not so easy when it's your family on the line.

In the PBS spiel, I said of my family: 'when things went downhill, we ... fled the country'. Those first four words – *when things went downhill* (and what more tritely perfect example of Australian understatement?) – papered over assorted bad things (death, suicide, dispossession, displacement, labour camp, starvation, subjugation), but the common coefficient to all this was a booklet of cheap, coarse, yellowish pages called the Declaration of Personal Background.

Saigon fell; the Communists took over. Law became ideology; your fate as a southerner was pegged to a Party line that twanged unpredictably in response to the internal and interpretive tensions of Marxist–Leninist–Stalinist–Mao Zedong Thought. Those few Communists who claimed to understand the theory spent their time contesting it with each other; the rest went about their usual business: classifying people. The Declaration was a brilliant originary outsourcing of work. It opened everyone's record: first you classified yourself class-wise (bourgeoisie, petite bourgeoisie, proletariat, peasantry) and then you accounted in detail everything you'd been, done, thought or associated with over a thirty-year time span. This led you to the next rung of classifications (puppet, lackey – imperialist or neo-colonialist subtypes – quisling, comprador, rightist, revisionist, reactionary, or – the catch-all – counter-revolutionary). You picked your poisons.

Then you repeated this process for every single person in your extended family, going back three generations. (Given the size of Vietnamese families, this typically involved over a hundred people.)

The Declarations would then be collected and cross-referenced against each other. You would expect to be cross-examined on what others had written about you. You would expect to be cross-examined against what you had written in your own earlier Declarations – for you were expected to regularly fill out new ones. People learned to keep things simple and consistent. They learned to apply the correct

Communist jargon. By way of countermeasure, Communists mandated interminable 'self-criticism' and 'struggle' sessions; they demanded you write extemporised, in-depth essay after essay. You had no choice. You had to keep producing the words that would be used to sentence you.

And so they were. The labels stuck, and they were fatal. They became your identity and your identity became your destiny. Based on these labels (*petit bourgeois, quisling*), my father was sent to a 're-education camp', where he was enslaved and tortured for three years. My grandparents (*neo-colonialist, compradors*) had their homes and businesses confiscated, their possessions commandeered, their savings devalued. Two of them suicided. My mother (*bourgeois, lackey*) fared better: she was merely relegated, with her baby, my brother, to a crowded garage that had once belonged to her family, and invited to pay her 'blood debt to the people' by relinquishing any rights, jobs, civic status or control over her future.

I'm reminded of a bit in Vasily Grossman's incandescent, excoriating *Life and Fate*. Our protagonist, a compromised intellectual in Stalin's Soviet Union, is (of course) filling in a questionnaire:

> Viktor wrote, 'Petit bourgeois'. Petit bourgeois! What kind of petit bourgeois was he? Suddenly, probably because of the war, he began to doubt *whether there really was such a gulf between the legitimate Soviet question about social origin and the bloody, fateful question of nationality as posed by the Germans.*

The italics are mine.

How far is the distance from 'legitimate' to 'bloody'?

Is this where you end up when you go too far?

~

Early in Malouf's *Harland's Half Acre*, some white boys come across a rock carving:

> Not far before the ruins there was a platform of rock. Aborigines had fore-gathered here, all the local tribes in their wanderings, and left crude rock carvings ... With their knees drawn up [the boys] would sit on warm stone in the very midst of it, among the sea-creatures and the flights of wallabies and paddymelons and every sort of bird; that other world would be all about them, abstracted into enduring lines that crossed and criss-crossed in an endless puzzle. The outline of a whale might be broken by that of a

bounding kangaroo, the separate orders of creation, sea-beast and land-beast, interpenetrating in an element outside nature – the mind of whoever it was, decades back, who had squatted here and with bits of flint or a sharpened stone made the clearing a meeting-place for separate lines of existence.

Malouf's books abound in numinous moments, but this one stands out for me. The rock carving is a work deeply in and of the world, made by many human hands. There is no separation of past and present, myth and materiality. This is archetypal Malouf in that everything is interconnected, everything liminal, on the verge of metamorphosing into a 'separate order of creation'. In *The Great World*, the hero, Digger Keen, says, 'Even the least event had lines, all tangled, going back into the past, and beyond that into the *unknown* past, and other lines leading out, all tangled, into the future. Every moment was dense with causes, possibilities, consequences; too many, even in the simplest case, to grasp.'

This is what identity looks like, Malouf is saying, if you must insist on it. It is, at its most basic, indistinguishable from existence, which is, in turn, infinitely complex – a network of tangled lines going every which way, through every part of being-in-the-world. These lines run in and out of place, time, genetics, culture, language, circumstance, accident, other people, all the happenstances of mind-life and dream-life. All a writer can do is stand in the midst of this monkey-puzzle mesh and pluck one line, then another, trying to happen on a harmonics that sounds right. Art comes (or it doesn't) from these soundings.

What is folly is imagining you could compact these lines into coherence, let alone sense – let alone representativeness. If my family history has imbued me with anything, it's the awareness that identity is complex, politics is complex. What a disappointment, then, that identity politics is so simplistic. I'm actually not unsympathetic to identity as politics, as political performance. There's a place, I think, for strategic essentialism: for the use of identity to create community, to centre sidelined voices, to defend 'standpoint epistemology', to bear witness and collate testimony – to redress structural inequity. As a person, a citizen, a comrade, I get it – I can even get with it.

As a writer, I find it profane.

Writers shouldn't be joiners, shouldn't be boosters or censors or mouthpieces – representatives – of anything but their own truths. They should protect, *at the exact cost of their art*, their artistic sovereignty. Because a correct literature is not a moral literature. Because without sovereignty, a writer is an instrument of a foreign power – truly a puppet, lackey, collaborator, quisling – and their work no more art than those millions of forced, falsified autobiographies written by my forebears. As soon as a writer can be *said to be* what others label them (from whatever intention), they're no longer – no longer allowed to be – entirely themselves.

'Entirely himself'. This is how Malouf describes Peter Porter, the Australian-born poet who spent his adult life as an expatriate in London. Belonging neither there nor here, he was instead 'made' by books (Auden, Pope, Donne), music (Mozart, Donizetti, Verdi, Bruckner, Bach) and, most of all, language. Malouf has written, of Christina Stead, that she 'belongs wherever she puts down her intelligence and allows it to take root'. Of Porter again: language is 'the only place he has ever been at home'. I might be projecting, but it feels to me as though Malouf might be projecting here.

English is my second language, my better language. It's the language better suited to my way of thinking – which was conditioned by it to think so. (It takes a mongrel, maybe, to know a mongrel . . .) I've never felt unwelcomed in it. Which is more than I can say for every place it's spoken. For me, the question of a writer's 'identity' – if it must matter – is answered, of course, by words. The true pedigree is linguistic. The true passport is imaginative. Writers should get some say in it. (Fancy that!) What matters is not what tribe or place *the person* was born to but what community *the writer* has made for themselves through reading, thinking, writing. Malouf's first name comes not from his Jewish or Melkite Catholic heritage but from Dickens – Copperfield, not King. His work, he wants us to know, is descended not from patchy family history but from the all-access traditions of so-called 'high art', and within them the writings of Homer, Hesiod, Horace, Virgil, Dante, Shakespeare, Dostoevsky, Tolstoy, Balzac, Hugo, Kipling, Lawrence, Kafka, Proust, Mann, Joyce.

There's a metaphor of Jean Rhys's I love in which she describes literature as a great lake to be continually fed. You pour yourself in, as a writer, you draw yourself out as deep as you dare. When Malouf praises overlooked Australian writers Kenneth Mackenzie and Frederic Manning by placing them in the company of Mann, Radiguet, Kafka, Musil, Hamsun, Camus and Beckett, it is the opposite of cringe – it is a carriage of justice, an action of equilibrium, of graceful re-centring. It is welcoming them into the middle of the lake, where the water, though darker, runs deepest.

PATRIA

There he is, in his fat golden tie, accepting the honour of his lifetime (so far). In his steady, high-pitched voice, David Malouf delivers his Neustadt Lecture at the University of Oklahoma, under the aegis of *World Literature Today*. He speaks of 'the power of language as a means of structuring, interpreting, remaking experience; the need to remap the world so that wherever you happen to be is the centre'. Later, he describes himself as 'a writer whose immediate world and material happen to be Australian'.

Happen to be. In the precise, lapidarian chisellings of Malouf's prose, this repetition takes on special significance. *Happen*, as in deed, but also as in happenstance. Something occurs and something is. This is the accepted order.

What occurs and is – in this instance – is *Australianness*. And here, at this point of deep concurrence, Malouf and I most meaningfully part ways.

~

Concurrence first. For his *Complete Stories*, a collection that gathers up at least three decades of work in the short form, Malouf picks his epigraph from Pascal's *Pensées*:

> When I consider the brevity of my life, swallowed up as it is in the eternity that precedes and will follow it, the tiny space I occupy and what is visible to me, cast as I am into a vast infinity of spaces that I know nothing of and which know nothing of me, I take fright, I am stunned to find myself here rather than elsewhere, for there is no reason why it should be

here rather than there, and now rather than then.

There is, in Malouf's work, an innate awareness of the *arbitrariness* of things. An awareness that each of us – and what art we might make – is a product of chance and random concatenation. That against the questions of why here and not there, now and not then – *there is no reason*. This is the first, and prerequisite, principle of moral awareness. For First Worlders, especially, it slows us from thinking we deserve what we've merely happened into: our bodies and brains, with what faculties they possess; our genealogical, cultural and linguistic inheritances; our situation in place and time, with its appurtenant advantages in health, education and technology; our array of advantages themselves.

So when he talks of himself as a writer who 'happens to be' Australian, Malouf is foregrounding the rule of accident. As his doppelgänger remarks in *Johnno*: 'If my father's father hadn't packed up one day to escape military service under the Turks; if my mother's people, for God knows what reason, hadn't decided to leave their comfortable middle class house at New Cross for the goldfields of Mount Morgan, I wouldn't be an Australian at all.' (This account is authenticated in Malouf's non-fiction and interviews.)

The point is: no volition is aroused in the fact of a writer's nationality, only in our spin on it. The fact itself is only as important as the writer – and we – decide.

~

What, then, of cases where volition *is* involved? A perfect case study comes to hand: J.M. Coetzee, who immigrated to Australia from South Africa in 2002 and naturalised in 2006. All evidence confirms he is both Australian and a writer. Not only that, he has written a substantial number of books here – including books set in Australia, featuring Australian protagonists, litigating Australian issues. At his citizenship ceremony, after making a pledge of commitment to Australia, he averred (albeit in generalised language) that any new citizen must 'accept the historical past of [his] new country as [his] own'. He even offered obiter courtesies about 'the free and generous spirit of the people ... the beauty of the land ... the grace of the city [Adelaide] that I now have the honour to call my home'.

So is Coetzee an 'Australian' writer?

That it's even an open question – and the most cursory consideration admits it is – speaks to a bankruptcy of basic agreement on what the question's asking. This, to me, speaks in turn to the underlying illogic of nationality. Coetzee is not an Australian writer because he doesn't pass some test of 'Australianness'. Okay then: what is this quiddity, how is it manifest, who gets to judge? Obviously passport-backed positivism isn't enough. Nor civic or cultural engagement – Coetzee, it's fair to say, knows and does more in this regard than most Australians (who never need prove they belong where they are). And it can't be because he wasn't born here, or hasn't spent enough time here, or is affiliated with another country: this applies to plenty of 'Australians' and 'Australian' writers.

There's a drift at work here, and it mirrors the drift of our current moment towards what might be catastrophised as the black hole of nationality. The closer anything comes to its event horizon – not excepting any universal principle or logic – the more deformed it becomes. Even among the cognoscenti (i.e. those who should know better), 'national interest' now liberally overrules other political or ethical imperatives (with 'national security' the trump); 'national unity' is unanimously invoked as pure good. To be called a 'true [insert nationality]' is both highest approbation and empty of normative meaning, as every nation is exceptional: every nation boasts the friendliest people (with 'free and generous spirit'), the deepest drinkers, the richest history, the most stunning natural beauty, the most beautiful beaches (if they have a coast) in the world, and all these claims are not just unchallenged, they are correct – because they are protocol.

Literature is not protocol. But it's not immune to it. If writers are constantly considered through the lens of nation, nationalism and its protocols will eventually refract logic, sense and proportion. Think of the mountain of scholarship on Malouf that treats solely or significantly with his Australianness. Hyper-specialisation has balkanised university departments and journals to the point where it's a specialisation in itself to consider literature 'comparatively' – that is, as readers and writers do: as part of an enterprise that is ongoing, accretive, atomistically autonomous, reflexive, conglomerate. The result is a kind of rigged exegesis, whose main mode is to bend books into thesis. *'Only an [insert label of choice] author could have written that'* is its catchiest jingle. And where that label is national, how effortless the transition into themes of contested identity, historical trauma, border politics, home and belonging. The articles write themselves!

Let's call this, off-handedly, the Kafka Fallacy. Per this approach, all insights and assertions about literature are ex post facto and therefore infallible. What do I mean? Kafka's writing, let's say, explored existential themes through fantastic motifs of nightmarish bureaucracy. It becomes self-evident, surely, that only a German-speaking Jew straddling the late nineteenth and early twentieth centuries / Bohemian-born writer / ex-lawyer with career experience in insurance / writer several times engaged but never married / writer with schizoid traits / tuberculotic writer – choose your own causality! – could have written it. Each of these propositions is irrefutably true (each having set its own truth conditions) and each is also fundamentally arbitrary. There are tons of tomes out there stuffed with this post-hoc preening and confirmation bias. What they ignore is the thing that most matters: the deep idiopathy of originality. Kafka's work could not have been imagined to exist – in all its genius and particularity – until Kafka came along and wrote it. His life led him to it, yes, but his life was convolved and exponentially complex in its causes and effects; it was – and is – unknowable. All serious art, in this way, is anomalous, is outlier art.

Johnno again: 'I had once found it odd, gratuitous even, that I should be an Australian. I found it even odder, more accidental, that I should be anything else.' To understand that arbitrariness is no impediment to the sanctity of *what is* is one definition of grace. One suspects that wherever else Malouf might have been born or raised, he would have, given the chance, arrived at the same restless and replete accommodation with that place. 'Temperament', he calls it. Nature unshaped by nurture. It's easy, employing the Kafka Fallacy, to imagine a Canadian or Rhodesian or Burmese Malouf writing *An Imaginary Life* or *Ransom*, word for word. But let's extend the thought experiment: what if these two books had been the only ones an Australian Malouf wrote? Neither was deemed, by the country's pre-eminent literary gong, to 'present Australian life in any of its phases'. Should the 'Australianness' of such a Malouf be correspondingly curtailed? What would it take for this hypothetical Malouf – or the actual Coetzee – to convincingly demonstrate his 'Australianness'?

Invariably, the quest to answer this question sees us shepherded into mythic terrain – a land bestridden by nebulous incarnations of 'national character' and 'national values'. As Les Murray memorably describes it: 'The Melbourne Cup and the Fair Go and a myriad gum trees live there, along with equality and Anzac Day and the Right Thing.' Fair enough. Sounds like a nice enough place. But folk myth tends to pull double duty as nationalist myth. And when nationalism finds it hard to find room for a celebrated, committed, white, fellow post-colonial citizen like John Coetzee, what hope for immigrants, or non-Anglos, or the growing number of Australians who subscribe less and less to such 'vernacular' self-conception?

~

A brief aside on the semiotics of hyphens.

Coetzee is never referred to as 'South African–Australian'. If, like me, he was born in one place and migrated to another, why should I be the one stuck with the hyphen?

What does the hyphen actually signify?

'Australian' is geopolitical fact (even if its appellation may be contestable).

'Vietnamese-Australian' is historical inference, compressing within it war, aftermath, the converse migration where left to right across the hyphen brings you East to West. Other hyphenations mean mixed parentage; not this one (in America, the offspring of local Vietnamese and American visitors are called 'Amerasians'; in Vietnam, these children are referred to as *bụi đời* – 'dust of life'). 'Vietnamese-Australian' also changes complexion depending on who's saying it. Say it about yourself and you're asserting hybridity or acknowledging heritage; having it said about you is being subjected to a racial charge. ('Vietnamese', which I get a lot in Europe, brings the charge right to the skin.) No matter how it's said, there's a subservience built into 'Vietnamese-Australian', a hum of model-minority conditionality.

(Note that Malouf is almost never referred to as Lebanese-Australian.)

'Asian-Australian' – bandwagoning 'Asian-American', which didn't even exist until the sixties – seems little more than fuzzy, clumpy identitarianism.

'Australian-Vietnamese' – doesn't exist. This is interesting, and surely bears thinking about. The politics of orientation, of ordinalism: people don't migrate from West to East; their stay is understood to be (indefinitely) temporary. As for West to West: by far the greatest numbers of migrants to Australia are from England and New Zealand and yet you rarely come across 'English-Australians' or 'New Zealander–Australians'. Coetzee is not 'South African–Australian' – he's just somewhat less than a dinky-di, true-blue Australian. There's a clubbiness at play here, coupled with a mutual accord that if you're from the Anglosphere, your origins are never superseded, let alone renounced – they remain your enduring birthright.

~

To me, Coetzee, like Malouf, (like me,) is a multivalent writer who *happens to be* Australian. As writers, both of them hold and are beholden to multiple 'lines' of affinity and identity – 'Australianness' is only one of them. And it is relevant only inasmuch as their work renders it so. I'm not being facetious when I say that writing this monograph has made me (feel) more 'Australian', just as writing a recent poem about Collingwood made me (feel) more 'Melburnian'. Intentionality – volition – has to be in the mix. Without it, any campaign of cultural nationalism can only be conscriptive. And I'd be useless, anyway, in any such campaign. 'When I look at the body of my writing', Malouf once said, 'I want to say to myself: "This is one person's attempt to give an account of what being an Australian is – this particular Australian.'" Despite the mildness of the language, what I feel when I read this is forcible constriction, coercion. I hardly want to give an account of being *me*, let alone me as any single, separable strand of identity.

Shirley Hazzard said of Patrick White that 'from the literary standpoint', his Australian-ness was 'both essential and irrelevant'. Only *essential*, I'd argue, because White himself made it matter: it was a lifelong irritant he kept agitating into fictive nacre. He was scathing about what he called the 'Great Australian Emptiness', scathing of complacent, falsely confident efforts to colonise it with the chimaera of 'national identity', scathing of his own monstrous and conflicted role in the campaign. When handing White his Nobel Prize, the Swedish Academy declared that his art had 'introduced a new continent into literature'. They could not have chosen a pithier way to prod the beast.

~

About this point I've got to check myself. Obviously, in opposing nationalism – and straining against the naked singularity of nationality – I'm indulging a prerogative granted to me by that same nationality. I'm an Australian citizen, and to be an Australian today is to have it pretty good: strong, stable democracy; peaceful, prosperous country. By every objective index, the average Australian is packed with privilege. On the hierarchy of needs, we base-camp at summit.

Another acknowledgement: national consciousness can be a positive force – especially during times of war and disaster. Part of me wonders if I am, in decrying it, debasing the sacrifice of my parents, who fought in a civil war waged over competing visions of nation. For them, nationalism wasn't an option but a necessity, a survival stance. They lost, here I am. (Here I am, among the chin-stroking cosmopolitan classes who can afford to treat nationalism abstractly, as something for Third Worlders.) Here we all are, in this small nation in this huge country, this island continent (we say 'overseas' while our British and American cousins say 'abroad') which – in comparison to almost every other nation on earth – has never known existential border war, civil war or revolution. (It should be obvious by now we're talking about 'modern' Australia.) How lucky are we?

I love this country. I feel lucky to be here. And I hate feeling at all compelled to say it – I hate the inferred ingratiation. I've been here long enough to know that as soon as you try to prove you belong, you don't. ('A mug's game, a mugger's game.') 'I actually like Australia very much', Malouf says in an interview, a small ridge of surprise in that 'actually' – it's not easy abandoning old defences. I want to belong, and I'm wary of this want in me. So (like Malouf, perhaps) I take my belonging in a spirit of play. The sporting analogy is apt: the high-grade tribalism, the manufactured all-or-nothing stakes and emotion in a match are real – and not to be belittled – but it's a bit pathetic, isn't it, even pathological, when people take it too seriously?

The better analogy, though, is closer to home. As a writer, like it or not, you're born into a nation. At least at the start, you can't choose it. It's a lottery. Your earliest reality is all Rawlsian veil of ignorance without any agency or election. Nation just ... *is*. In this way, it's not unlike *family*. Family environs you, brands you, enfleshes you. It conditions your beliefs and biases, your thoughts and your ways of thinking.

And it's utterly arbitrary.

It's also unfair. You're plonked in a tribe without consent. Once there, coercion frames your existence. You're cornered in a space pulsating with other people and odd laws, dependency and taboo, love and dread, consummation and quarantine. Asymmetry is the operative norm. There's no meaningful concept of justice that could possibly account for who goes into which family, or what goes on inside any family.

And it's irrational. You're *meant* to be too close to family to be fair-minded about it. You're *meant* to care too much. You're *meant* to be hyper-critical, then hyper-defensive when anyone else dares criticise. Most of all, for your own sake, your own sanity, you're meant to accept it as it is. Bless it for being.

As a writer, my take on nation is basically the same as my take on family. Acknowledge that it's always there, in the bones. Acknowledge its arbitrariness. Own the bad as well as the good, not as process of blame, but of truth. Don't get wholly sucked in: keep your self – or some part of it – sovereign. And even in the midst of mooning and moaning over *who* you are, remember *that* you are. That's where the real wonder is. It's people and places that are sacred, remember, not borders.

We don't police people's kinship with their own families. Nor should we police anyone's – least of all any writer's – 'Australianness'. ('Un-Australian', as epithet, is pure dominance behaviour. It's telling that what it attacks – violence, gangsterism, non-neighbourliness, unkindliness, cowardice, wankiness, wowserism – is usually *also* demonstrably uber-Australian.)

Nations, like people, contain multitudes. And late colonial nations hold the habits of self-hate deep inside their nationalism. We don't ask people to define themselves constantly against their families; let's not ask writers to do so constantly against their nations. Let's not make it the first thing we mark about them. For some people, family is a huge obsession; for others, background. Some families are consciously mythopoeic, reinforcing themselves through legend and lore and incanted ancestry; others, not so much. It's all good! Let's give writers the same freedom – without threat of exclusion or attenuation – to consider questions of national identity, national culture, national politics – *or not*. As they see fit. Or not.

PERIL

Long before 'Australia' was a British 'possession', it was an act of imagination. Speculation about a great southern land exists on record as far back as Aristotle. It's still thrilling to see the first printed mention of 'Australia' in an astronomical treatise published in 1545, in the middle of an exquisite twelve-wind rose. On different maps, in different musings, this southern *terra* was variously *ignota*, *incognita*, *nondum cognita* and, latterly, infamously, *nullius*. Unknown, yet to be known, no-one's. Laid out like a virgin for a good thorough civilising.

Despite hazy reports of first contact with Indonesians and Chinese, 'Australia' has always been a European dream, deeply tied up with

European naval-gazing. For centuries, European ships pressed south, searching for land, while back home their people ventured fantasies about what they might find and what it might mean. Portuguese, Dutch, Spanish and French all came, or came close; then the English finally slapped up against the south-eastern coast and claimed the entire *nondum cognita*. In Peter Porter's 'On First Looking Into Chapman's Hesiod', he teases, 'who would have thought / Australia was the point of all that craft / Of politics in Europe?' Indeed, it must have been a blow to many an excitable mind when the Brits – to the question of what a new continent might augur by way of example, or even utopia – answered *penal colony*.

Hesiod, as it happens, is much on Malouf's mind. In an interview with his friend and fellow writer Colm Tóibín, then subsequently in his

Neustadt Lecture, Malouf likens the situation of a contemporary writer in Australia to that of Hesiod in Boeotia: '*at the beginning*' (echoing, of course, Genesis). The land, he marvels, is 'a real gift' to the writer, as 'everything' – or 'the real making' – is 'still to be done'. D.H. Lawrence, in *Kangaroo*, looking through similar eyes at this country, sees: 'Tabula rasa. The world a new leaf. And on the new leaf, nothing.'

Tabula rasa. (*Terra nullius.*) What a gift, what a temptation, for a writer of ambition! Australia, annexed through invasion and occupation, nevertheless supine and primed for 'full possession', as Malouf puts it, by poets and fictioneers. (Penal colony indeed.) In his Boyer Lectures, he asserts:

> What we did when we came here was lay new knowledge, a new culture, a new consciousness over what already existed,

the product of so many thousands of years of living in, and with the land.

Parapraxis by preposition again: the relationship of European consciousness to the land is dispensed as *over* (not *to*, or *against*, or *through*, let alone, as attributed to the indigenous population, *in* or *with* the land). In Malouf's short story 'The Only Speaker of His Tongue', the English language is said to 'set all this land under another tongue'. ('Language', of course, coming from the Latin '*lingua*' for 'tongue'.) The English tongue, with its 'gift for changing and doing things', kills off the old land. I'm guessing Malouf allows himself uncharacteristic bluntness here because he's speaking in fiction, in implied translation, through the arm's-length persona of a Norwegian lexicographer. Laid *over*, set *under* – the metaphor is one of benign smothering, snuffing out. And as apt as it may be to describe the action of colonialism, I find it describes, even more arrestingly, the way Malouf handles the subject of colonialism in his work.

There is, in Malouf, a tendency towards wholeness. He creates tension through binaries (self/other, mind/body, past/present, human/non-human, human/world, European/Australian, Australian/Aboriginal, civilised/primitive, centre/periphery, adult/child, experience/innocence, inside/outside, white/black, fate/free will, etc.) and then yearns, and seeks, naturally and inexorably, to syllogise them – often through lyrical transcendence – into reconciled wholes. At bottom, this is his entire method. At its best, it results in writing that is surpassingly beautiful, moving and profound.

This therapeutic cant, however, bangs up badly against the concrete blocks of colonial history. Malouf would have us write our way towards a 'collective spiritual consciousness that will be the true form of reconciliation'. Without new literature, new myth, without imaginative re-creations, he argues, the wounds of colonialism cannot be healed. But an imported language is no more impartial or innocent than an imported law. British possession was legitimised by British law; violence more than took care of the rest. Ours is a land done in by deeds *and* deeds. In *Remembering Babylon*, Malouf refers, in passing, to a massacre of Indigenous people as a 'dispersal'. The euphemism abjures itself – but it is still a euphemism.

This, I think, typifies the paradox of 'national' literature. Once you set out to purify the dialect (plagiarising T.S. Eliot) of your nation, to justify its existence (A.D. Hope), you enthral yourself to the idea of a national narrative. And narratives are dangerous things. They contort and concoct and clean up in the service of concertment. Malouf hints at this in *Harland's Half Acre*, where Frank Harland, the painter, is depicted as a kind of holy fool, while his father, the storyteller, is a trickster – a fraud who defiles sacred breath with each word. My preceding account of high school, my family's history – things didn't happen like that – not really, not only. Narratives will do just about anything to make things cohere. Writers especially should not be trusted with them.

Even the best writers. Malouf has called for the making of a new Australian mythology – a new national sacred – pointing to the Aboriginal capacity for adaptiveness, reminding us of 'the extent to which Aboriginal notions of inclusiveness, of re-imagining the world to take in all that is now in it, has worked to include us'.

As if that work wasn't done with a gun to the head. As if work so done could be said to validly express the attitude of the doer. Let's be clear: Malouf, as citizen, co-authored the 1999 draft Declaration of Reconciliation; his intentions are only creditable. But it's hard for me to believe, pace Malouf as writer, in his concept of 'full possession' of a place. (*An Imaginary Life*: 'It is our self we are making out there, and when the landscape is complete we shall have become the gods who are intended to fill it.') And it's impossible for me to get behind a notion of 'reconciliation' that exhorts further imaginative 'possession' of an already expropriated place. That isn't palimpsest – it's overwriting. It's just another dimension of dispossession. And if our new national myth can only be rooted in – and feed off – our oldest open wound, how is it meant to heal us?

~

Writing is world-making, and world-making takes violence. Malouf would be aware that cosmogonic myths are overwhelmingly gorged on murder and rape, mutilation and dismemberment. The parallel with colonialism is not accidental. The word 'Europe' comes from the Ancient Greek *'Érebos'*, meaning 'darkness'; the European civilising mission spurts forth from a heart of darkness where white men rear themselves up as gods over the inferior races.

By pitching Australia as 'a real gift' to writers – 'with the real making still to do' – Malouf openly tincts his work with neocolonial motive. It's a genteel form of frontier madness: why take fifty acres (thirty more for wife and each child) when you can take possession of the whole bloody continent? Malouf's body of imaginative work, which he's forthright about curating, stakes out the largest moments and themes in Australian history: first contact, colonial settlement, the Western Front, the fall of Singapore, Changi, the Thai–Burma Railway, the myths of the white man gone native, the bushranger, the prisoner of war. World-making takes ego. And make no mistake, David Malouf – as mild and modest as he's famed to be – and no doubt is in person – is megalomaniacal in his work. He names, more than once, Goethe, Mann and Hugo as true voices of their national literatures, personifications of their languages, musing that this conceit 'has no equivalent in our literature culture'. (Interesting, that '*our*', given it was a talk in London to English PEN.) Meanwhile, for half a century now, he's been carrying out his own sedulous, stupendous project of nation-writing. Writing is 'public dreaming', Malouf has said; if so, his dreams are become public works. And when he's not dreaming our nation, he's increasingly crafting and clarifying it in argument. Malouf is probably our living writer most concerned and perspicacious about what it means to be an Australian writer. His Boyer Lectures were subtitled 'The Making of Australian Consciousness'. The man is, need we remind ourselves, a National Living Treasure.

Which leads me, finally, to wonder: what am I missing? Why can't I get interested in Malouf's campaign of cultural nationalism? I'm as avaricious, I reckon, as the next Aussie scrivener; as smitten by the opportunity to make myth. Why does 'Australianness' as call to linguistic arms or literary subject feel so inert – so alien – to me? Could it be as simple as my usual reactance to corporatising thought? To policed parochialism? Or could it be that this jingoism of national identity recalls too closely, for me, the asterisked boosting of 'ethnic' identity? Whatever the answer, it doesn't lie with the new trendy label, 'transnational', or the old soiled one, 'cosmopolitan'. Both tags acquiesce to an order I dispute and disclaim. And no, I can safely say I'm less 'deracinated' than simply aware that to be rooted arbitrarily is, as we say in these parts, to be rooted.

The plain answer, I fear, is this: 'Australianness' is alien to me because I'm still alien to Australia.

~

The birth of Australia as a nation coincided almost exactly with the passage of the *Immigration Restriction Act 1901*. This legislation codified what everyone knew, as summed up by Prime Minister Edmund Barton:

> I do not think either that the doctrine
> of the equality of man was really ever

intended to include racial equality. There is no racial equality. There is basic inequality. These races are, in comparison with white races – I think no one wants convincing of this fact – unequal and inferior. The doctrine of the equality of man was never intended to apply to the equality of the Englishman and the Chinaman.

Later three-time PM Alfred Deakin (I was vice-captain of Deakin House at school) wrote of:

our distrust of the Yellow races in the North Pacific and our recognition of the *entente cordiale* spreading among all white men who realise the Yellow Peril to Caucasian civilization, creeds and politics.

Thus was the White Australia policy kicked off – on the platform of Yellow Peril.

(Pre-Federation colonies did their bit with a plethora of anti-'Chinese' Acts.) W.K. Hancock, our magisterial national historian, called the White Australia policy 'the indispensable condition of every other Australian policy'. PM Billy Hughes (in 1919) described it as 'the greatest thing we have achieved'. Arguing for conscription in 1916, he equated the 'spirit of Australia' with 'the spirit of our race'. One world war later, PM John Curtin (in 1938) affirmed that Australia would remain forever 'an outpost of the British race'. ('We intend to keep this country white,' PM Stanley Bruce declared in the interim, reassuring a skittish public that Australia was still 98 per cent British.) The nation's first immigration minister, Arthur Calwell, said (in 1947), 'We have twenty-five years at most to populate this country before the yellow races are down on us.' (This from the same man who said, 'Two Wongs don't make a White.') And PM Robert Menzies (in 1955), having mulled over 'oriental countries', blithely said, 'if I were not described as a racist I'd be the only public man who hasn't been'.

Know thyself! The point I'm making is simple: being non-white, I've always been – will always be – an outsider in Australia. There'll always be some reason why someone's neglected to loop me into the *entente cordiale*. The White Australia policy may have been abolished in the '70s but all non-whites know it's as deeply situated in our DNA as our Western inheritance. (Yes, I said, and will say, 'our'.) We're not over it. Maybe things will be different for my kids – I hope so – though I'm not unduly optimistic. Think of it this way: the proportion of American history in which blacks were not legally dehumanised (under slavery or segregation) matches up closely to the proportion of our history post–White Australia policy. Who would dare argue that American racism towards black Americans is a thing of the past?

For people of colour, moreover, the reality is exclusion not only from belonging but from the *binaries* of contested belonging – European/Australian, Australian/Aboriginal, white/black. Indigenous Australians may be execrably treated in a thousand ways but they're generally safe from accusations of 'Un-Australianness'.

And here's the thing. All that said, I don't see myself as a victim of Australia's past. Nations (like families) are not fair. They're all sorts of trouble and wrong. It should be possible to see, and call out, and work towards repairing wrong without being defined by it. Sook and snarl are ultimately as limiting as cringe. There's power and beauty in what is, and there's agency in exclusion. Part of this attitude in me is temperamental, I suspect, and some part must spring from background: I was born in a country that proudly (if head-scratchingly) takes as its national icons things brought in or radically co-opted by colonisers: *áo dài, bánh mì, phở,* romanised script with diacritical marks. Whatever works! (This might also explain my puzzlement at a Western progressivism that happily amputates its own intellectual heritage for being unwoke.) Whiteness theory posits that the dominance of whiteness in Western nations arises from its being the unacknowledged, invisible norm, but this is not at all true for refugees, who clearly see and acknowledge whiteness as power but who hope and trust that such power may be checked by self-declared political principles and practices. Work with what you've got! As a refugee myself (what unassailable safety to write those words! what authority! what impunity!), I'd hate to be admitted into a Western nation where white identity is under siege, and then be press-ganged into the militant 'multicultural' ideology that's seen as the enemy. Better things to do. Other fish to fry. Leave me out of it, please.

~

David Malouf's essay 'The Kyogle Line' is one of the few places he writes in a personal vein about race. It's a revealing essay, more for what it omits than what it says. He writes about his paternal grandfather, who came to Brisbane in the 1880s from 'greater Syria; itself then a province of the great, sick Empire of the Turks'. At the time, 'greater Syria (as opposed to Egypt and Turkey proper) was declared white – but only the Christian inhabitants of it'. It's under this regime of almost farcical arbitrariness that

Malouf's never-named grandfather scrapes in. He never makes an effort to learn English, and never naturalises, which leads to his being interned when Lebanon becomes a Vichy dependency.

His son, Malouf's father, on the other hand, 'was as Australian as anyone could be – except for the name. He had made himself so. He had played football for the State, and was one of the toughest welterweights of his day'. Elsewhere, Malouf writes of his father establishing his Australianness 'with his fists'.

Just beneath the surface of nation, violence – always violence.

Is it a stretch to hazard that Malouf may have inherited (or at least self-inculcated) this urge to establish his Australianness? In 'The Kyogle Line', Malouf belatedly realises that his father must have 'grown up speaking Arabic as well as he spoke Australian … But I never heard him utter a word of it or give any indication that he understood.' What extraordinary discipline – and, one imagines, extraordinary loss – to have so interred your parents' language. And what extraordinary danger must have been intuited to necessitate such discipline. I think of my children, what it would communicate to them were I to never again speak Vietnamese, never even show – to *my* parents, say – that I understood it. In 'The Only Speaker of His Tongue', our lexicographer describes the passing down of language through the generations: 'We recapture on our tongue, when we first grasp the sound and make it, the same word in the mouths of our long dead fathers, whose blood we move in and whose blood still moves in us. Language is that blood.'

Language is that blood. What, then, might it signify that Malouf speaks and reads four languages – none of which is Arabic? That, in his writing, he has transfused the blood of his 'long dead fathers' out of his body? That he has, in fact, exsanguinated himself of this entire (Lebanese, greater Syrian, Middle Eastern) half of his heritage? I know it shouldn't matter. And mostly it doesn't. It hasn't. The man should be free to write whatever he wants, however he wants, on his own terms. The work he has given us is tremendous. But still, to me, the spilled blood screams. The site of excision remains raw, livid. And the terms of Malouf's work invite a heuristic of making (and making sense of) present through past, selfhood through inheritance. In calling for a new Australian sense of itself, Malouf has been searching and stirring about its Western and British inheritances; he has made it his life's work to keep delving into this 'matter of Australia'. In one long essay, he laid out the many ways in which Australia (and he) was 'made in England'. Malouf is, incontrovertibly, a writer in the business of identity.

Only not, it seems, one half of his own.

Here's a crazy thought. Could it be that whiteness, for David Malouf, is both blindingness and camouflage? That out of temperament, intuition, reflex, survival and ambition, he has suppressed his brownness – as his father suppressed his Arabic – in order to 'pass' as white? This sounds preposterous, I know. And I'll probably get in trouble for it. But the thought, once thought, is hard to unthink.

In his poem 'Notes on an Undiscovered Continent', Malouf writes, 'The nineteen tongues of Europe / migrate to fill a silence'. Only the tongues of Europe wag. By private erasure as well as public policy, Australia is white. (Alfred Deakin: 'Other races are to be excluded

by legislation if they are tinted to any degree.')
Only a white Australian (the young, ambitious,
half-Lebanese Malouf would have understood)
could hope to forge in the smithy of his soul the
uncreated conscience of 'his' race. Only a white
Australian could assert standing to 'make' this
nation – to fully 'possess' this land. To advance
Australia fair.

In *Johnno*, Dante's friends decamp for
Europe even as he decides to stay in Brisbane.
'I was determined, for some reason', he says, 'to
make life reveal whatever it had to reveal *here*,
on home ground, where I would recognise the
terms.' Such complacent unconcern, such assur-
ance. Dante/Malouf expects to belong where he
is. It's *home ground*. But no non-white, I expect,
no matter how long, how deeply rooted in Australia, would so casually describe it that way.

~

The action of 'The Kyogle Line' is simple: Malouf and his father walk a Coffs Harbour train platform in 1944 and come upon a crowd gathered around three caged prisoners of war:

> The three Japs, in a group, if not actually chained then at least huddled, were difficult to make out in the half-dark. But looking in at them was like looking in from our own minds, our own lives, on another species.

This is David Malouf writing in 1985, at the centre of his career, the height of his powers. A writer who considered his second book, *An Imaginary Life*, to be his last – 'an old man's summing up, a late meditation on death, on continuity and change, the possibility of transformation' – and every book afterward to be a 'filling in'. And what filling in since – what curiosity and empathy, how prodigious his traversals of time, place, sex, age and class. Here was a writer who dared venture, in fact, into the consciousness of animals, of the natural world – even the cosmos.

And yet here he is, stopped short, finally, by this other – Asian – 'species'. By a 'vast gap of darkness' – between the crowd and the Japanese men. Between Australia and Asia. Malouf registers: 'The moment you stepped out of the crowd and the shared sense of being part of it, you were alone.' The boy witness could have known no better. But the mature writer, *this* mature writer, forty years on, alone with his memory and conscience, in full possession of hindsight and decades of ethical and imaginative praxis, might have been expected to look at these men and see them as more than 'other' or grotesque 'object', to at least assay the 'possibility of transformation'. I will admit that reading this account (especially straight after reading Malouf's stock 'culture shock' account of a trip to India) left me in a state of mild dejection. Forty years on from White Australia and not even a glimmer, from our most conciliatory writer, of imaginative 'reconciliation'.

~

Something else. The stunned, tense silence of these Australians staring at three 'Nips' – it feels familiar to me. In more than a personal way, in a way that has nothing to do with race. After a while, I realise the déjà vu is aesthetic: it mirrors almost exactly the attitude – and language – of a different category of Australian writing. Not about people, but about the landscape – specifically 'the bush'.

Remembering Babylon gives it form as:

the abode of everything savage and
fearsome, and since it lay so far beyond
experience, not just their own but their
parents' too, of nightmare rumours, super-
stitions and all that belonged to Absolute
Dark.

The land harbours 'illimitable night'. 'Even in
full sunlight it was impenetrable dark.' In *Johnno*,
Australia is 'what begins with the darkness at
our back door'. 'What the vastness of Australian
spaces evokes', Malouf declares in his Neustadt
Lecture in Norman, Oklahoma – the most
tornado-prone area on the planet – 'is anxiety'.

Settler Australians, of course, had reasons
to be anxious. Their public dreaming was its
own strain of prairie madness—cum-colonial
nightmare – haunted by irretrievable Albion,

revanchist first peoples, an unforgiving land. They were not invited and they were never welcomed. The bush became their giant imago of fear and guilt. Always there, just on the other side of the sill, just beyond the last European syllable – *a vast gap of darkness*. Even a century and a half later, in a large city, the young Malouf would find himself drawn to the crawlspace underneath his family's stilted weatherboard. The mysterious dark between European edifice and immemorial earth. As though, even then, he knew his work must issue from this anxious space.

And here I'm forced into another admission. Try as I might, I have never been able to properly access this anxiety – this shared apprehension of Australia, described by Malouf in 'Jacko's Reach', as 'the dark unmanageable'. A lifetime here, and I'm still outside even this primal sense of being outside. When Malouf praises Slessor's poem 'South Country' as a breakthrough in Australian consciousness, I can admire its technicality, but feel as emotionally removed from its portentions of a 'monstrous continent of air' with 'black / Bruised flesh of thunderstorms' as I do from the hokiest bush ballad. The Australian landscape, to me, is many things, but it is not monstrous, and it is not malevolent. I mark no ancient fear in it – it poses nothing but itself.

And that's when it hits me. For non-Anglos, non-Europeans, non-whites – *whiteness* is our 'bush'. Whiteness is our surrounding, seething reality, the autochthony we yearn for and can never achieve. (If we seem to come close, it's only ever because we're 'industrious and imitative'.) Whiteness is the perpetual engine of our anxiety. And this, in the end, is perhaps the most enduring lesson I've received from

Malouf. He and I are both self-made, but here, in this country, he's able to pass, has passed. (And, I believe, it may have cost him.) I cannot. I'm tinted by my face, cruciated to my hyphen. And I realise too that this is the land's real gift to me. It's okay. I no longer have to try.

BOOKS BY DAVID MALOUF

NOVELS

Johnno (1975)

An Imaginary Life (1978)

Fly Away Peter (1982)

Child's Play (1982)

Harland's Half Acre (1984)

The Great World (1990)

Remembering Babylon (1993)

The Conversations at Curlow Creek (1996)

Ransom (2009)

SHORT STORY COLLECTIONS

Antipodes (1983)

Untold Tales (1999)

Dream Stuff (2000)

Every Move You Make (2006)

The Complete Stories (2007)

POETRY

Bicycle and Other Poems (1970)

Neighbours in a Thicket: Poems (1974)

Poems 1975–76 (1976)

Wild Lemons: Poems (1980)

Selected Poems 1959–1989 (1994)

Guide to the Perplexed and Other Poems (2007)

Typewriter Music (2007)

Revolving Days (2008)

Earth Hour (2014)

An Open Book (2018)

NON-FICTION

12 Edmondstone St (1985)

A Spirit of Play: The Making of Australian Consciousness, Boyer Lectures (1998)

Made in England, Quarterly Essay (2003)

On Experience (2008)

The Happy Life, Quarterly Essay (2011)